MARK TWAIN
You Never Knew

BY JAMES LINCOLN COLLIER

Children's Press®

A Division of Scholastic Inc.

Library of Congress Cataloging-in-Publication Data
Collier, James Lincoln, 1928-
  The Mark Twain you never knew / James Lincoln Collier ; [illustrations by
Greg Copeland].
     v. cm.
  Includes bibliographical references (p.   ) and index.
  Contents: A writer's boyhood — Earning a living — Roughing it — Writing
the classics — The masterpiece.
  ISBN 0-516-24430-2
  1. Twain, Mark, 1835-1910—Juvenile literature. 2. Authors, American—19th
century—Biography—Juvenile literature. [1. Twain, Mark, 1835-1910. 2.
Authors, American.] I. Title.
  PS1331.C564 2004
  818'.409—dc22

                         2003028305

Illustrations by Greg Copeland
Book design by A. Natacha Pimentel C.

Photographs © 2004: Art Resource, NY/Alinari/S. Maria delle Grazie, Milan,
Italy: 51; Bridgeman Art Library International Ltd., London/New York: 12, 13
(Museum of the City of New York, USA), 71 (New York Public Library, USA), 75
(Private Collection), 69 (The Stapleton Collection); Corbis Images: 67, 76 bot-
tom (Nathan Benn), 1, 23, 31, 33, 35, 38, 47, 52, 57, 62, 64 (Bettmann), 8, 70
(Buddy Mays), 30, 76 top (Museum of the City of New York), 17 (Leonard
de Selva), 58; Hulton|Archive/Getty Images: cover, 4, 39, 40, 43, 46; Library of
Congress: 12; North Wind Picture Archives: 15, 36, 76 center;
PictureHistory.com: 20.

Published in 2004 by Children's Press, an imprint of Scholastic Library Publishing.
Published simultaneously in Canada.
Printed in the United States of America.
1 2 3 4 5 6 7 8 9 10 R 13 12 11 10 09 08 07 06 05 04

CONTENTS

Chapter 1

A WRITER'S BOYHOOD

MARK TWAIN IS PROBABLY THE best-loved of American writers. This nation has produced many great authors. Herman Melville, who wrote the famous novel Moby Dick, is certainly one of the country's most admired novelists. Henry James's books are still widely read. More recent novelists, like Ernest Hemingway and William Faulkner, are known around the world.

Twain at age thirty-five formally dressed for a lecture. In most cases he dressed without much care, sometimes going around with his shirttail out.

But Mark Twain is unquestionably the most American of them all. His celebrated characters, especially Tom Sawyer and Huckleberry Finn, could not have come from anywhere but America. Ernest Hemingway said, "All modern American literature comes from one book by Mark Twain called *Huckleberry Finn*." Hemingway was exaggerating a little, but not very much.

One reason Twain was such an American writer is that he based much of his work on his own experiences. All writers do this in one way or another, but Mark Twain constantly used things in his work that had happened to him, his friends, or other people he knew about. He said of *Tom Sawyer*: "Most of the adventures in this book really occurred; one or two of them were experiences of my own, the rest those of boys who were schoolmates of mine."

He did not use these events exactly as they had happened. He often exaggerated them or twisted them around to make them more interesting. This creates a problem for anyone who wants to study Mark Twain's life. We can never be sure that the stories he told about himself are exactly what happened.

For example, his book *Roughing It* is supposedly about his adventures in the mining camps and rough towns of the West. But people who have studied this period of his life can show that many of the stories he put into *Roughing It* couldn't have happened as he wrote them. Most likely they happened to somebody else or happened at another time and another place. Twain never denied that he rearranged facts to make better stories. Later he said, "When I was younger I could remember anything, whether it happened or not; but I am getting old and soon I shall remember only the latter"—the things that didn't happen. Twain was making a joke, as he usually did, but there is truth in it.

So, to understand Mark Twain's writing, we need to know about his life. But it should be noted that we cannot always count on his writings to fairly describe what he actually did.

Fortunately, Twain has been of great interest to students of American literature. Many people have studied his life and his books. Many books have been written about him. We can be sure of the basic facts.

He was born in a tiny village in Missouri called Florida, on November 30, 1835. His father, John Clemens, had at one time or another been a judge, a lawyer, and a storekeeper. He had been quite well-off by the standards of the time and place. However, by the year Mark was born, John Clemens had lost most of his money. Thereafter he would try all sorts of schemes for getting rich, but none of them worked. Mark Twain would grow up with very little money.

Mark was actually named Samuel Langhorne Clemens. But, the world came to know him as Mark Twain—we will learn why later—and we will call him by that name in this book to avoid confusion.

The most important person in Mark's life as a boy was his mother, Jane. He thought she was wonderful, even though she punished him a lot for getting into mischief. She had red hair, as did Mark. "She had a slender, small body, but a large heart—a heart so large that everybody's griefs and everybody's joys found welcome in it, and hospitable accommodation. . . . She felt a strong interest in the whole world and everything and everybody in it."

The house Twain grew up in in the little town of Hannibal, Missouri. It was comfortable and large enough for a family, although two or three of the children would normally share a room. The house is now a museum displaying items related to Mark Twain.

One time a cruel, tough man was beating his grown-up daughter. The young woman ran to Mark's mother, who took her into her house. The father came roaring up and demanded his daughter. Small as she was, Mark's mother stood before the door and wouldn't let the angry father in. The man raged, but Jane Clemens shouted right back at him, telling him what a bad man he was. Soon enough the man grew ashamed of himself, apologized, and slunk away.

A second important person in Mark's life was his uncle John Quarles, who owned a farm near Florida. Even after the family moved away from Florida, Mark would often return in the summer to visit the Quarles farm. He loved the place, "the solemn twilight and mystery of the deep woods, the earthy smells, the faint odors of the wild flowers. . . ." Like most boys, he also loved the food that was served at country meals: "Fried chicken, roast pig; wild and tame turkeys, pheasants, partridges, prairie-chickens; biscuits, hot batter cakes, hot buckwheat cakes, hot 'wheat bread,' hot rolls, hot corn pone," and much more. The sights, smells, and tastes of the American countryside would fill his books.

However, as pleasant a place as Florida, Missouri, was, John Clemens did not do well there. In 1839, when Mark was four, the family moved to Hannibal, a much larger town on the Mississippi River that was growing rapidly. John Clemens did not prosper in Hannibal either, and he died there when Mark was eleven. But American readers gained a great deal, for Hannibal was where Mark Twain grew up. The experiences of his boyhood in Hannibal are everywhere in his books, especially his most famous ones, *The Adventures of Tom Sawyer* and *The Adventures of Huckleberry Finn*.

Later on Mark wrote about how he had been a sickly child for the first seven years of his life, always taking one kind of foul-tasting medicine after another. But he soon became a strong, vigorous boy, although smaller than average. He had brothers and sisters, whom he also put into his books, but the main character he put in was himself.

The truth is that Mark Twain, even as a small boy, liked to show off. He wanted to be the little star of the family, and he was. A liking for the spotlight is a good trait for a writer and lecturer to have.

But Mark was not just a show-off. Even as a boy he had a reckless independence of spirit that got him in trouble. His mother wrote to somebody that "He drives me crazy with his didoes [tricks], when he is in the house, and when he is out of it I am expecting every minute that some one will bring him home half dead." An independent spirit, too, is a good quality for writers to have, for they need the courage to say what they truly feel.

When he was a boy this independent spirit proved to be risky. Once there was an epidemic of measles in Hannibal. At that time measles was a very serious disease, which children often died from. Mark was filled with fear that he would catch measles and die. "Every night a sudden shiver shook me to the marrow, and I said to myself, 'There, I've got it! and so I shall die!'" To end the suspense, one night he crept out of the house and slipped into the bed of a boy badly ill with measles. Of course Mark got sick, and for awhile it seemed that he might die. Fortunately, he recovered.

The life of a boy growing up in Hannibal was built around the Mississippi River. It was a mile wide there, and every day the great steamboats of the time rolled past it or pulled up to the docks to land passengers and freight. All the boys in Hannibal greatly admired the famous riverboat pilots with their fancy clothes and their proud swagger. The Mississippi River would play an important part in several of Mark's books.

Inevitably, the children in town all learned to swim in the great river, although most of them had been told not to for good reasons. Mark almost drowned in the

Mississippi several times. Later in life he recalled a woman "plucking" him from the water "by the hair of my head when I was going down for the third time."

He skated on the Mississippi during times when it froze. Once he and another boy were skating on the river when they heard the deadly creaking sounds of ice breaking up. In terror they raced for shore, for if they fell into the freezing water they would surely die.

But the ice was now broken into large chunks that tipped and swayed as the boys jumped from piece to piece. Finally they neared shore. Here there was a stretch of open water. Mark made it safely across on a chunk of floating ice, but his friend fell in. The friend struggled to shore, but came down with a serious illness that left him deaf for life.

In time Mark became an excellent swimmer. Once he was on a boat when his hat blew off into the water.

In Twain's youth, roads in America were poor and few in number, especially in the half-settled western states. Most travel was by water. The Mississippi River was a very busy place with steamboats constantly passing by, along with all sorts of smaller rafts, canoes, and rowboats.

The boat was a long way from shore. A sensible person would have let his hat go, but Mark was not rich, and he liked his hat. He dove into the water, caught up to the hat, and began the long swim through the windblown water to shore. On land spectators gathered, thinking they had seen the last of Mark Twain. But Mark made it safely to shore, carrying the precious hat with him. Although he surely wanted to save his hat, we have to believe that Mark was showing off a little, too.

Growing up in Hannibal could be a lot of fun, but there were dark sides to it. For one thing, Mark began smoking and chewing tobacco when he was quite young, probably about ten years old. He gave up chewing tobacco after awhile, but he went on smoking cigars and pipes all day long for the rest of his life. Not as much was known then about the dangers of smoking as we know today, but Mark knew that smoking as much as he did was not good for him. When he got married he promised his wife that he would quit smoking, but he never did. In fact, he lived to a good age, but he probably would have lived longer if he had not smoked so much.

For another thing, growing up, Mark often felt guilty about the mischief he got into. He was, he believed, something of a bad boy. And it was certainly true that his independent spirit at times got him into trouble.

Making matters worse, at the time children in Sunday school were always being told that they were likely to burn in hell for little things, like lying or talking back to their parents. Mark Twain never really got over the idea that he did bad things too often. In fact, he was really no worse than most people, and a lot better than many. He was an honest man who usually behaved decently toward the people he knew. Later in life some people he got into a business deal with lost money on account of it. Twain was not legally bound to pay the money back,

Marble games came into popularity after Twain's boyhood but were a very common form of entertainment for children in the latter half of the nineteenth century and the first half of the twentieth. In this game the object was to snap one of your marbles so that it knocked other marbles out of the circle.

but he went on a long lecture tour to earn extra money, and paid it in full. A lot of people would not have been so fair. But even so, Mark Twain often felt more guilty about small things than other people would have.

Finally, there was the whole question of slavery. Slavery and the problems faced by African Americans were big questions in America in Mark Twain's day. It is an important part of many of his books. We cannot discuss Mark Twain's work without considering slavery.

Missouri, when Mark was growing up, was a slave state. Slavery was normal there. For a while Mark's father had a slave girl to help around the house whom he sometimes whipped when she was not quick enough to obey. He also had a little slave boy to do chores whom he often shouted at fiercely and sometimes beat.

In the South there was nothing unusual about that. Most Southerners—in fact most Northerners, too—believed that blacks were not smart enough to take care of themselves and needed to be kept in slavery for their own good. It seemed to many Southerners, and some Northerners, that the Bible permitted slavery. As a boy, Mark Twain accepted these beliefs.

But in the South, it was usual for black and white children to play together. Mark knew black people very well. And as he grew up, he began to change his mind about slavery. Blacks, he came to see, were no worse and no better than anyone else. In time African-American characters found their way into his books. One of the most famous ones was the black man, Jim, who made the celebrated trip on the raft down the Mississippi River with Huck.

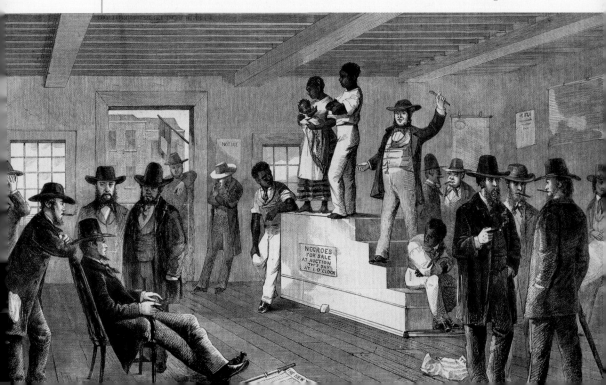

Slaves were bought and sold like animals, as shown in this drawing of a slave auction. However, in the upper South where Twain lived, it was usually considered wrong to sell slaves when it could be avoided. Even there it happened, though, especially when a slave owner died and the estate had to be broken up.

As an adult Twain came to hate slavery, and he would work to help some young blacks get educations. *Huckleberry Finn* would not be the only writing by Twain concerning the problems of blacks in America.

So Mark Twain had a very American upbringing, quite different from the boyhoods of people growing up elsewhere in the world. He ran barefoot on the dusty streets of a small American town, on the banks of a great American river, listening to the hooting of the glamorous steamboats—an American invention—going to and fro. He ate American food like corn pone and wild turkey, gathered nuts and berries in the woods, joined in coon and turkey hunts. And he lived amidst slavery, an institution that would be a major concern for Americans for much of the country's history.

American Twain was. But if anyone had said that this mischievous boy growing up in a small town on the Mississippi would become one of his country's greatest writers, everybody would have burst into laughter. He hated school and never studied any more than he had to—although, curiously, he always did well at spelling. He was far more interested in rambling in the woods or swimming in the river when he wasn't supposed to than in reading books or discussing ideas. Why would anyone possibly expect that such a boy would decide to be a writer? And in fact, he took a long, winding path to get there. If any number of things had been a little different, there might never have been a Mark Twain, or a Huckleberry Finn.

Chapter 2

EARNING A LIVING

IN MARK TWAIN'S TIME FEW YOUNG people went to school beyond the age of fourteen. Many did not make it even that far. At fourteen, boys were expected to go to work. Boys living on farms, as most Americans did then, became full-time farmers. Boys like Mark, who lived in towns, were expected to find jobs and bring money home to their families. At that time girls were only beginning to work outside the home.

Mark Twain at around the age of forty, when he had become well known as a writer and lecturer.

At fourteen, or younger, girls stayed home to help around the house. They took care of the younger children, learned to bake bread and pies, sew clothes, care for chickens and pigs, and do the many jobs people of those days did at home. There was plenty of work for all.

So Mark would go to work—but at what? By chance, his older brother Orion had been apprenticed to a printer in St. Louis, a growing city about a hundred miles down the Mississippi from Hannibal. Nobody is sure why Orion became a printer. It was considered a respectable trade to be in, for it was connected to books and literature, but it was certainly not a path to riches. It was decided that Mark would become a printer like his brother.

The job his family found for him was at a local newspaper, the Hannibal *Courier*. Under the apprentice system, Mark would work for several years for nothing but his meals and his clothing. In exchange he would be taught the printer's trade. As it turned out, the food was never very lavish, and the clothes were his boss's secondhand suits, which were far too big and gave Mark "the uncomfortable sense of living in a circus tent," as he later put it.

In those days, there were no computers to automatically set type, nor high-speed presses like the ones that print today's newspapers. Mark worked from a case of letters. This was a flat box divided into many small compartments, each containing a lot of copies of one of the letters of the alphabet. The person "composing" the type held in his left hand a small box called a compositor's "stick." He quickly picked the letters of the words he was setting from the case and lined them up in the stick. The words had to be set backward, so they would come out right when they were printed. A trained compositor soon learned where all the letters were in the case, so he could snatch them out one at a time without looking. A good compositor could set type very speedily.

When the lines of type for a story were set, they were locked into a frame the size of a page. This frame

The rotary printing press sped up the printing process and made modern newspapers possible. Nonetheless, the old-fashioned flatbed press remained in use for smaller jobs well into the twentieth century.

was in turn locked onto a press. The type was inked, and paper was pressed onto the type.

Usually several frames of type were locked onto the press together. They were arranged so that when the paper was folded the right way, the pages would come out in the correct order. As readers can guess, setting and printing pages this way to make a book took a good deal of time.

A printing shop like the one Mark apprenticed in did all sorts of work. It printed advertising posters, wedding and birth announcements, restaurant and hotel price lists, pamphlets, and books. But the most interesting work was the newspaper. Apprenticing on a newspaper proved to be very important for Mark Twain.

Without radio, television, movies, or the Internet, people depended on newspapers for much of their information and entertainment. Slow transportation made it impossible for newspapers to cover a wide territory, therefore each little town had to have its own paper. Newspapers carried articles about important events like elections, shipwrecks, and murders as newspapers do today, but they also printed poems, short stories, humor, and serious essays. If one newspaper came up with a particularly good story or essay, many other newspapers would reprint it. Usually the writer of the story got paid only the first time it was printed, but if a story was reprinted in hundreds of papers, the writer might become well known. This, in fact, would eventually happen to Mark Twain.

Mark soon became a good printer. For one thing, his natural skill at spelling was very helpful. For another, he seemed to have a feeling for words, although that was not obvious at the time.

Mark worked for the Hannibal *Courier* for about a year, and then moved on to a newspaper started by his brother Orion, the Hannibal *Journal*. On this newspaper he began to write. We do not know why he decided to write. He was, after all, a boy who had always preferred to be outdoors rather than studying. Partly it had to do with Mark's liking for showing off—writing pieces for his brother's newspaper was a good way to call attention to himself.

But there was more to it. As he grew up a little, Mark began to realize how poorly educated he was. There was, clearly, a great deal about the world that he didn't know. And so he set out to educate himself by reading whatever books he could get his hands on. Books at the time were expensive. Most families did not have many shelves of books, as some families do today. Mark borrowed books from friends, from printers, from libraries when he could find them. In time he studied all sorts of things. Eventually he taught himself to read both French and German.

People who like to read often think about doing some writing. This was the case for Mark. His wish to improve his education began to push him in the direction of writing. He was not yet thinking about becoming a full-time writer. That seemed to him, still a teenager, too great an ambition. But at least he could write little pieces for his brother's newspaper.

Being a mischievous sort of person, he chose to write mischievous pieces—humor, to be exact. His first story was very short and was called "A Gallant Fireman." It told about an apprentice who, when the shop next door caught fire, "gathered the broom, an old mallet, the wash-pan and a dirty towel" to save from the flames. He had the apprentice use the roughest kind of slang: "If that thar fie hadn't bin put out," and so forth. For the rest of his life Mark would write about people who behaved foolishly—often himself—and spoke in slang or dialect. Perhaps more important, almost by instinct, he chose to write about the way people really talked, behaved, thought, and felt. He would exaggerate for comic effect, but from the beginning he was focusing on the actual things that people did. "A Gallant Fireman" is a good example. It was certainly foolish of the apprentice to save a broom and a dirty towel from the fire instead of more valuable things, but that is the way people often act when they are in a sudden panic.

Thereafter, every few weeks or few months, Mark would write a little something. Two of these brief stories were picked up by other publications. Mark was thrilled by this. It was one thing to get published in his brother's newspaper, it was quite another to have other papers want to use his writings. Fifty years later Twain said that seeing these pieces in well-known publications "was a joy which rather exceeded anything in that line I have ever experienced since."

Over the next few years Mark Twain traveled to New York City, Philadelphia, and St. Louis, always working as a printer. He became skilled at this trade, and might well have made printing his life's work, perhaps ending up running his own newspaper. He continued to occasionally write short pieces for the newspapers he worked for, some of which were printed elsewhere. But he had no plans to make a career for himself as a writer. It did not seem to Mark that he could possibly earn a living by writing.

By 1857, he was twenty-two years old and had been a printer for about eight years. He was growing bored with doing nothing but setting type and pulling the lever on a printing press. He wanted a greater challenge. The career he now chose was a natural one: steam-boating. The steam engine had been invented in England, but Americans had developed the steamboat. In Twain's time much of America was still covered with forest, desert, and plains. Roads were poor, often just wagon tracks through a forest. By far the easiest way for people and freight to travel was by water, either up and down the coasts or along the many lakes and rivers abounding in America.

Right from the beginning, sailing ships had carried American products like cotton, tobacco, timber, wheat, and much else from port cities like Boston, New York, and Charleston all across the world. As Americans spread out in a westward direction across their own country, their products traveled along rivers like the Ohio, the Mississippi, and the Delaware to port cities on barges, flatboats, and even canoes.

But while it was one thing to float a barge *down* the Mississippi or the Delaware to New Orleans or Philadelphia, it was quite another to get a loaded barge back *up* such rivers against the current.

A boat driven by a steam engine solved this problem. The steamboat for use on rivers was rapidly developed. By the time Mark was born the steamboats were bringing great prosperity to river cities like Cincinnati, Pittsburgh, St. Louis, and many others. Steamboats grew bigger and fancier. Some had huge dining rooms for passengers. They were painted in gaudy colors and their brass fixtures were polished to a high shine. There was enormous glamour attached to the steamboats.

However, they could be dangerous. Sometimes when a steamboat captain was trying to make good time or was racing another steamboat for fun, the steam pressure in the engine would grow too great and

Farmers along the Mississippi River earned money by cutting wood for use by steamboats. Here a steamboat pulls up to the bank to take on a load of wood.

the boiler would explode, scalding many people and perhaps engulfing the boat in flames. Rivers, too, were treacherous. Often boats ran into underwater sandbars, floating trees, or the wrecks of other ships—and sank.

The person responsible for steering the ship safely through these obstacles was the pilot. He had to know the river well and see the danger spots where something might be lurking beneath the surface of the water. Mississippi steamboat pilots were much admired. They made a lot of money, dressed in elegant clothes, and stayed in the best hotels between trips. Mark Twain had grown up on the Mississippi admiring the pilots he had seen at a distance from the dock at Hannibal. The life of a riverboat pilot was full of risk and adventure. It would be far more interesting than setting type day after day. Besides, what better opportunity to show off than to be a Mississippi riverboat pilot? So he apprenticed himself once again, this time to a well-known riverboat pilot named Horace Bixby. Years later Mark Twain would make Bixby the most celebrated riverboat pilot in history when he put him into his classic book, *Life on the Mississippi*.

Mark's job under Bixby was to "learn the river." The Mississippi was full of dangerous places where rocks or sandbars lay just under the water. Depending on the season and recent weather, the river might be high at times, low at others. On top of that, the rush of waters along the banks was always carving away at

There was much competitive spirit among steamboat men, who often challenged each other to races as they went up and down the river. But sometimes when they pushed the boats too hard the boilers blew up, killing many of the passengers.

the land and changing the shape of the river. Mark stood with Bixby taking notes while Bixby pointed out dangerous spots and safe channels. Soon he was allowed to spin the great wheel himself, according to Bixby's instructions. At first he was stunned when he realized how much information he had to learn by heart. But gradually he learned. And in time he became a licensed Mississippi riverboat pilot himself. Now it was his turn to swell around in fancy clothes, ignoring the admiring looks of boys just like the one he had once been. No thoughts of becoming a writer crossed his mind then.

Mark's success on the steamboats encouraged his younger brother Henry to try steamboating as well. Mark got Henry a job with him on a boat called the *Pennsylvania*. Mark was not with Bixby this time, but with a pilot named William Brown, "a surly, stupid, and ignorant" man, according to Mark, who made life miserable for the people under him. Once Henry was supposed to tell Brown to pull toward shore in order to land the boat at a certain point a mile or so downriver. Brown was a little deaf and didn't hear Henry pass on this instruction. The boat went by the landing spot. But Mark had been there, and he had clearly heard Henry give Brown the message.

Later Brown denied that Henry had told him anything. Henry said, "I did tell, Mr. Brown."

"It's a lie!"

Mark said, "You lie yourself. He did tell you."

Brown picked up a huge chunk of coal and started for Henry. Instantly Mark grabbed a heavy stool and jumped in. He knocked Brown down with the stool, and then leapt on him and began pounding him with his fists. Brown struggled free and raced for the wheel, for the *Pennsylvania* was running full speed down the river with nobody steering.

Mark Twain's pilot's license. Twain was proud of having been a river pilot and carefully preserved his license long after he had become famous as a writer.

After that Brown would not work with Mark anymore. When the *Pennsylvania* reached New Orleans, Mark got off. Henry stayed aboard as the *Pennsylvania* went back upriver. A few days later the boat's boiler blew up. The scalding steam instantly killed most of the passengers who happened to be on deck and some of the crew. Brown's body was never found.

Coming up the river in another boat, Mark heard about the dreadful accident. He saw in the river corpses and parts of the boat his brother had been on. In terrible fear he kept asking people along the way for details. Some of the survivors had been taken to a hall in Memphis, Tennessee, to recover from their injuries or die. When Mark got to Memphis he hurried to the hall where the injured were lying. There he found Henry, his body wasted and covered with burns. Mark knew instantly that his brother would die, and he collapsed to the floor.

Despite the great loss of his brother, Mark Twain continued to work on the riverboats. Then, in 1861, the American Civil War began. Both Union and Confederate sides wanted control of the Mississippi River. It became the scene of much fighting. In May 1861 Mark rode as a passenger on the riverboat up to St. Louis. There a Union cannon fired at the boat. "A shell exploded directly in front of the pilot-house," he wrote, "breaking a lot of glass and destroying a good deal of the upper decoration." Riverboat traffic, except for warships, came to a halt. Mark Twain's career on the river was over—and American literature was changed forever.

The Mississippi steamboats revived after the Civil War, but they did not last much longer. By that time a new invention, the railroad train, was spreading rapidly across the nation. Trains were a cheaper and faster way to travel than were steamboats, and gradually the river trade dwindled. But in time Twain would immortalize the Mississippi steamboats in his books.

He got one more thing out of the riverboat days. Mark Twain got his name. In order to judge the depth of the water, a seaman would drop a weight tied to a rope into the river until it touched bottom. Marks on the rope told him how deep the water was. Each mark indicated a fathom of depth—about six feet. *Twain* means two. *Mark twain* thus showed a depth of twelve feet, usually water deep enough for a riverboat to travel through safely. Mark told several stories about how he took this particular name. We are not sure what the truth is, but he certainly made the name famous.

An artist's idea of an attack by Northern troops on a Southern position on the Mississippi River in Missouri. Twain was not in this particular skirmish, but was caught up in a similar one not far away. He did not enjoy the experience.

Chapter 3

ROUGHING IT

WITH THE RIVERBOATS STOPPED BY THE Civil War, Mark had once again to look around for a new career. It still did not occur to him to try to make his living by writing. In fact he had not done much writing during his years on the river, only four or five short pieces. He was much too busy learning the river to write.

As a Southerner, Mark tended to sympathize with the South in the Civil War. For a couple of weeks he served in a rebel army company, which was soon disbanded. By this time Mark Twain had come to disapprove of slavery and was not a strong supporter of the South. He decided it would be best to get away.

Twain in 1864, at the time he was a reporter on the Virginia City Territorial Enterprise.

Once again his brother Orion led the way. Orion had gotten a job in the brand-new Nevada Territory. This part of the West was booming. In 1847 the United States had beaten Mexico in a war and had taken control of California and much of the land in the Southwest. Almost at the same moment, gold was discovered in California. By 1861, when the Civil War closed the Mississippi to the riverboats, wagon trains were carrying thousands of Americans across the plains to farm the rich, fertile lands of California and the Northwest or to hunt for gold, silver, and other minerals in the western lands.

Panning for gold. The gold hunters would scoop up some soil from the bottom of the stream and then slosh the water around, gradually washing away the dirt. If the panner was lucky there would be a few flakes of gold in the pan each time he panned.

This new American land was being organized into territories, which would eventually become states. Valuable minerals, especially silver, had been discovered in the Nebraska Territory. Mark decided he would go out to the Nebraska Territory with Orion to hunt for silver. He had saved eight hundred dollars from his piloting work, a good amount of money in those days. With that as a stake, he was sure he would find a fortune in silver. In this belief he was no different from thousands of other Americans, mostly men, who went west at this time to seek their fortunes. A few found amazing lodes of gold and silver and became millionaires.

Settlers enter Nebraska looking for land to homestead. Land was easily available, but this prairie soil was very tough and hard to work. A lot of immigrants to the area preferred to look for silver.

Most lost their savings, went broke, and returned home sadder but wiser. Mark Twain would find no silver in Nebraska, but he would find something far more valuable—a career as a writer.

In July 1861 Mark and Orion set off for Nebraska. For the next year Mark worked at a number of jobs, but mainly he prospected for silver. Digging in the stony hills was hard work. He often ate nothing but beans and bacon for days at a stretch. He lived in small cabins with roofs that leaked when it rained. He slept rolled up in blankets on the ground. And all the time he dreamed of wealth—a grand mansion in San Francisco with a billiard room, a greenhouse, two acres of lawn, and a coachman to drive him places.

It was only a dream. All around him were tough men who stole, fought, sometimes killed each other. He wrote home, "Man named Gebhart shot here

A mining camp in the Sierra Nevada Mountains after the discovery of silver there in 1859. Mark Twain enjoyed the life there with its gambling halls and saloons and had great fun writing about the West.

yesterday while trying to defend a claim on Last Chance Hill. Expect he will die."

So weeks went by, and then months, and Mark found no silver. His savings ran out. He took casual jobs to keep himself going. One of the things he did was to write short pieces for a newspaper in Virginia City, Nevada, called the Virginia City *Territorial Enterprise*. The paper printed news from various areas around the West, especially stories about finds of gold and silver. The editors also wanted stories about murders and robberies, as newspaper editors still do today.

Mark Twain was still as full of mischief as he had been at the age of ten. Some of the pieces he wrote for the *Enterprise* were comical. Readers enjoyed them, and in August the editors of the paper offered Mark a full-time job at twenty-five dollars a week—not nearly as much as he had earned as a riverboat pilot, but enough to live on. So off he went to Virginia City.

In 1862, when Mark arrived, Virginia City was a boomtown. Two years before, it had been "a straggle of tents and shanties," as Mark described it. Now elegant stores and offices were rising, some of them made of brick. Wagons and stagecoaches crowded the streets. Fifteen thousand people, mostly men, lived there. Soon there would be three theaters, some churches, several newspapers, many saloons and dance halls. There was plenty of money around. Those who had none expected that they soon would be rich, for underneath Virginia City ran the famous Comstock lode, "the richest body of ore ever discovered in America," according to Mark.

By his own account Mark arrived in Virginia City very "rusty looking," wearing "a slouch hat, blue woolen shirt, pantaloons stuffed into boot tops, whiskered half down to the waist, and the universal navy revolver slung to my belt." Somebody who knew him well at the time gave another description:

> *He had the curly hair, the aquiline nose . . . an eye so eagle-like that a second lid would not have surprised me—of an unusual and dominant nature. His eyebrows were very thick and bushy. His dress was careless, and his general manner one of supreme indifference to surroundings and circumstances. He spoke in a slow, rather satirical drawl, which was itself irresistible.*

The *Enterprise* was the biggest paper in Nevada. It was the perfect place for Mark to work, for the editors wanted to produce a lively, entertaining paper.

It printed the news, such as reports of the Civil War raging back east, stories of mine collapses and explosions, rich gold and silver finds, and articles on local politics. But there were plenty of lighthearted stories as well.

The paper was particularly fond of running hoaxes—wild inventions meant to fool the unwary reader. One of these hoax stories was about a cooling device for travelers in the hot western plains that froze the inventor to death. The mischievous Twain soon contributed a hoax of his own, called "The Petrified Man." The supposed petrified man had been dead for centuries and had turned to stone. But if you read the story carefully you realized that the petrified man was winking one eye and thumbing his nose at passersby. Not everybody read the story carefully. Several newspapers in the West picked up the story and ran it as real.

The editors of the *Enterprise* liked Mark's mischief. They didn't object when he said that one politician was "long-legged, bull-headed, whopper-jawed."

This drawing shows men underground working the famous Comstock lode. As the miners dug into the lode, they had to continually prop up the earth above with heavy timbers.

They did not complain when he said that a particular night session of the legislature was "in many respects superior to a funeral." He always referred to a competing journalist as "The Unreliable," even though the man was his good friend.

In general, Twain would dress up a story on any subject with funny lines and observations. With his great imagination and sense of humor, he could turn an ordinary political report or story of a gold discovery into an amusing article. Other newspapers started picking up his stories. The name *Mark Twain* spread around. Within a year he had become the best-known humorist in the West.

But it was not just his writing. He was popular, too. Though many people were annoyed by his frankness and mischievous ways, most people liked him. He had his black moods, but usually he was humorous and fun to be around. He could make a joke about anything. In a story about a serious earthquake in San Francisco he wrote, "Heretofore our earthquakes . . . have been distinguished by a soothing kind of undulating motion, like the roll of waves on the sea, but we are happy to state that they are shaking her up from below now."

He was very energetic and talkative. Sometimes when he got wound up on a subject he would leap up from the dinner table and stride around the room talking and waving his napkin.

In June 1864 Mark moved to San Francisco to work on a newspaper there. He also contributed reports to the *Enterprise* and wrote humorous articles for a literary paper called the *Californian*. These pieces were successful, and the editors of the *Californian* asked him to write one for them every week. These articles helped him to create his humorous style.

Now important eastern journals, like the New York *Weekly Review*, began to run his stories. The *Review* referred to him as "one of the cleverest of the San Francisco writers." Mark was developing a national reputation.

During this time in San Francisco Mark Twain wrote a story that brought him his first real fame. The story is known today as "The Celebrated Jumping Frog of Calaveras County," although it originally had a different name. The story is simple enough. Mark probably got part of the idea for it from one of the miners he had known in Nevada. It is about a frog whose owner thinks it is a great jumper. Another man bets the owner that the frog is not as good a jumper as the owner believes. When the owner of the famous

In 1855, San Francisco was a rough place, but the money pouring in from the gold and silver mines, shipping, and cattle ranching was making the area wealthy. By the time Twain reached it, San Francisco had hotels, theaters, and concert halls along with bars and dance halls.

frog is away for a little while, the other bettor feeds the famous frog a lot of lead shot, so that it cannot jump. He wins the bet.

There is not much to the story. It is Twain's manner of telling it that makes it so good. He had by now discovered one of the secrets of humor is to tell some very outlandish tale in a straightforward manner as if it were deadly serious. The contrast between the strange story and the serious manner of telling it creates the humor.

"The Jumping Frog" was published in the New York *Saturday Press* in November 1865. Many other newspapers and magazines reprinted it. One reporter said that it "had set all New York into a roar." James Russell Lowell, a famous literary critic of the time, said that "The Jumping Frog" was the finest piece of humorous writing ever produced in America. Twain now wrote his brother Orion that he had a "call" to literature

Twain's story about "The Jumping Frog" brought him his first fame. This sketch shows him astride the frog, waving his cap to the crowd.

"of a low order—i.e., humorous. It is nothing to be proud of, but it is my strongest suit."

Mark was still not making much money, however. Newspapers and magazines did not pay well, and magazines that picked up stories from elsewhere usually did not pay at all. In January 1866 a newspaper sent Mark out to Hawaii to report on the islands, which most Americans knew little about. The reports Mark sent back were popular, but once again they did not earn him much money. Mark then decided to give some lectures on his Hawaiian experiences.

Today this would seem like an odd way to make money. However, in Mark Twain's day lecturing was very big business. With no movies, radio, television, recorded music, Internet, or electronic games, going out to hear a lecture was an important form of entertainment. People lectured on all sorts of subjects, including politics, literature, and social questions like slavery.

Mark rented a lecture hall for a certain night and advertised a lecture on Hawaii. As the time for the lecture approached, he later wrote, he "thought of suicide, pretended illness, flight." The night arrived. "Before I well knew what I was about, I was in the middle of the stage, staring at a sea of faces, bewildered by the fierce glare of the lights, and quaking in every limb . . . the tumult in my heart and brain continued for a full minute before I could gain any command over myself."

The lecture was a great success. One person later described it as follows: "His slow drawl, the anxious and perturbed expression of his visage, the apparently painful effort with which he framed his sentences . . . and the surprise that spread over his face when the audience roared with delight . . ." were a great part of the comic effect. Mark was using a lesson he had learned earlier—to present a strange situation in a solemn, deadpan delivery. In that one lecture he made more than he could have made in three months of writing for newspapers. For the rest of his life, whenever Mark Twain needed quick money, he would go out on a lecture tour.

Mark now felt ready to go back east and take on New York. He made an arrangement to write feature articles on New York for a California paper. In New York he gave some lectures and arranged to have his famous "Jumping Frog" story published in a book with some of his other comic pieces.

Then he learned about a pleasure cruise that would soon depart from the United States to visit famous places abroad. Pleasure cruises of this kind are common today. In Twain's time they were new. He persuaded the California paper to send him on the cruise, which was quite expensive.

In June 1867 the cruise ship, called the *Quaker City*, sailed. In his writings about the long trip, which took several months, Twain was his usual playful self. He made fun of the passengers. He called one of them a "wide-mouthed, horse-laughing young fellow" who had brought his own compass to make sure that the ship's compass was correct. Another passenger showed pictures of "the places where we expect to go." The first picture he showed was of a cemetery.

But mainly Twain made fun of the foreign places they visited. At the time, many Europeans considered Americans to be rough, uneducated people who knew nothing about music, books, and art. To get even, Twain took great pleasure in making fun of the famous sights of Europe. Compared to the majestic Mississippi, the famous Arno River in Italy was "a great historical creek." The celebrated painting *The Last Supper* by Leonardo da Vinci looked like "an old fireboard." In Constantinople the dogs were "mangy and bruised and mutilated. . . . " The great mosque Saint Sophia was "the rustiest old barn in heathendom."

Of course Twain was being unfair about many of these things. Other people found Saint Sophia spectacular.

Twain knew he was being funny. But in truth, he believed a good deal of what he said. One of his biographers said that to Twain "ancient Rome might have been glorious, but it was also dead." America was alive.

Whatever Europeans might have thought about Twain's opinions, Americans doted on them. Two days after the ship got back to New York, a publisher wrote Twain a letter asking him to write a book about the voyage. He wrote it. Called *The Innocents Abroad*, it became a bestseller. It is still fun to read today. Mark Twain, at thirty-five, was now a famous author.

The Last Supper painted by the Italian painter Leonardo da Vinci. Twain poked fun at the Europeans in The Innocents Abroad *by comparing the famous painting to a decorative cover for a fireplace.*

Chapter 4

WRITING THE CLASSICS

MARK TWAIN HAD GREAT SUCCESS with "The Jumping Frog" and with his travel book, *The Innocents Abroad*. He was finally sure that he could make a living as a writer. He would not be a writer of great tragedies, like William Shakespeare, or poems filled with complex ideas, like John Milton. He would be "only" a lowly humorist. But it would have to do.

For Twain, in any case, it was important to make money—as much of it as he could.

Mark Twain in formal dress at about age fifty-five. Twain usually dressed in a rumpled white suit, but had to wear formal clothes on certain occasions.

We remember that he had been raised poor. He had made good money as a riverboat pilot for two years. For the rest of his life he had earned small wages as a printer and a newspaper man, and even smaller wages as a prospector for silver. He wanted to be wealthy.

He had another reason for wanting money. During the long trip on the *Quaker City* he had become friendly with a young man named Charley Langdon. Charley was the son of a wealthy coal dealer from Elmira, New York. During the course of the *Quaker City* trip Charley had shown Mark a picture of his older sister, Olivia. She was very beautiful, shy, and ten years younger than Mark. He was very attracted to her. After the trip Mark went to Elmira to visit Charley. He met Olivia. She turned out to be not only beautiful, but very refined.

In those days, if you wanted to be accepted by wealthy people of society you had to have refinement. That meant knowing the right clothes to wear for each occasion, having excellent table manners, and knowing how to make pleasant conversation that put other people at ease. Refined ladies never swore, were usually very religious, drank little or no alcohol, did not smoke, did not cross their legs, did not sprawl around on a sofa, but always sat with their feet together on the floor. This kind of refinement was hard on people, especially women, and in time it would mostly disappear.

Mark Twain was definitely *not* refined. He had grown up in a little river town among rough people and had worked among even rougher people on the riverboats and in mining camps. He had seen life in the raw as a newspaper reporter. He sometimes drank beer and whiskey, and he smoked cigars and pipes almost all the time. He swore when he was out with his male friends. He liked to play jokes on people, and he was a sloppy dresser. He was certainly not the right sort of person for the shy, refined Olivia Langdon.

Mark visited the Langdons in Elmira for two weeks. At the end of his stay he asked Olivia to marry him. She refused. But she said he could write to her as if she were a sister—meaning that he shouldn't write romantic letters. He did anyway. Slowly Olivia came around. First she said she could never love him but that she would try to help him reform his ways. On another visit to Elmira, Mark gave one of his amusing lectures. According to Twain, Olivia began to love him when she saw how amusing he could be on the lecture platform. There was undoubtedly more to it than that, but she decided she wanted to marry him.

Olivia's parents were not at all sure they wanted their elegant daughter to marry this rough newspaper man with his western ways. Jervis Langdon, her father, asked Mark for the names of some of his friends who might speak in his favor. The letters he got back from Mark's friends said that Mark was "a brilliant, able man, a man with a future," but that he "would make about the worst husband on record." Mr. Langdon then asked Mark if he had any other friends who might speak well of him. No, Mark said, he didn't.

Then, according to a biographer, "Jervis Langdon held out his hand. 'You have at least one,' he said. '*I* believe in you. I know you better than *they* do.'" He agreed that Mark could marry his daughter, and in time Mark and Olivia were married. It proved to be a happy marriage, although there were times when Mark felt the need to get away from so much refinement for a bit, and would go off on a lecture tour or a writing assignment.

Some critics have felt that Olivia cramped Mark Twain's writing style too much. It is true that Mark read to her most of what he wrote before it was published. If she thought parts were too rough or coarse he would usually take them out. But in fact Mark wanted to be more refined. Most people of his time believed that they ought to be well mannered and careful about not drinking too much, cursing, or being too boisterous. Mark had never had much education or training in good manners. Here was his chance to learn. So it was not just that Olivia wanted to reform Mark, but that he himself wanted to know how society people behaved. He trusted Olivia's judgment about this.

Olivia had grown up in a wealthy home, and Mark wanted to make sure she would always have the things she was used to. They would need servants, horses and carriages, well-kept lawns and gardens. They would have to entertain friends and relatives. In those days wealthy people often made long visits of weeks, or even months, to each other.

Mark agreed to all of this. He was not being forced into

Mark Twain with his daughters Clara and Susie. The deaths of Susie and another of his daughters at early ages were partly responsible for the darkness of his last works.

a lifestyle he didn't like. He wanted to live like a wealthy and successful person. But it would take money, and he would have to earn it by writing.

His first big success had come from writing about something he had experienced—his travels that had resulted in *The Innocents Abroad*. Eastern Americans, and Europeans as well, were interested in the Wild West of America—the Plains Indians riding bareback on their ponies to hunt buffalo, the legendary cowboys, the rough little mining towns, the swashbuckling gold millionaires in the streets of San Francisco.

Mark Twain at a formal dinner party. Mark liked the idea of being refined, but he much preferred going out with male friends to smoke and drink and tell rowdy stories over going to formal dinner parties.

It was a strange and romantic world to people living settled lives in large cities like Boston, Philadelphia, London, and Paris.

Mark decided to write a book about his experiences in the West. He started it in 1870 and finished it the next year. It is called *Roughing It*. The book is made up of stories of his days in Nevada and California as a miner and newspaper reporter. The stories are mainly based on real people and events, but as usual, Twain exaggerates things or twists them around to make better stories of them. In a few cases the stories, as far as historians can tell, never happened at all.

In many cases Mark makes himself the butt of the joke. He presents himself as an innocent young man, inexperienced in the ways of the West. Time and again the more experienced people he meets take advantage of him.

In truth, by the time Mark went west he was not nearly as young and inexperienced as he makes it seem in *Roughing It*. On the first page of the book he says "I had never been away from home," but of course he had traveled a lot as a printer and had spent several years as a riverboat pilot. But the comedy came from the idea of the innocent youth being swindled by experienced westerners.

One typical story from *Roughing It* is about Mark being tricked into buying a horse that wouldn't let anyone ride it. The horse bucks Mark and anyone else who tries to ride it off within minutes. In the end Mark has trouble giving the horse away. Undoubtedly the story is based on a kernel of truth. Twain was not an experienced rider and would have had trouble with horses. But the humor lies in the exaggeration of his inexperience and the wildness of the horse.

Roughing It was another great success. What was he to do next? Mark was still writing short articles and stories, and from time to time over his life he would put together collections of the best of these. He was also lecturing, as he would do occasionally until the end of his life. But he knew that fame and glory, to say nothing of money, came from books.

Nearly everything he had written to this point had been either newspaper reports or based on his own experience, however loosely. He now wrote a novel called *The Gilded Age*, in collaboration with another author. Even Twain in time decided that it was not very good. However, it sold well enough.

The Gilded Age contains some characters based on people Twain had known in his youth. Next he turned to a book that would be mainly based on his own life as a boy growing up in Hannibal, Missouri. Actually, Twain had probably started this book earlier, perhaps in 1870, although we are not sure about that. He wrote at least a chapter of it in 1872. Then, in 1874, he took up the story again. He called the boy in the story Tom Sawyer.

The Adventures of Tom Sawyer was written from Mark Twain's heart and mind. At the time he was working on it he said that he was "wrapped up in it and so dead to anything else." He was "pumping" it out of himself.

An illustration from a later edition of The Adventures of Tom Sawyer, *showing the famous whitewashing scene. In the book the fence is described as being thirty yards long and nine feet high. However, that was how despairing Tom saw it. In Mark's experience it was probably more like the one in this picture.*

At one point "the story made a sudden and determined halt and refused to proceed another step." He was, as he said, pumped dry. He had to take some time off from it to refill his emotional tanks before he could go on.

Mark wrote *The Adventures of Tom Sawyer* for everybody, adults as well as children. However, today it is considered a children's book. Probably most young Americans read it at some time while they are growing up. It is unquestionably one of the most famous of all children's books by an American—indeed one of the most famous in the English language, as popular as the *Oz* books, and *Alice in Wonderland.*

Among other things, it contains what is probably the best-known scene in all of children's literature. Very early in the book poor Tom is made to whitewash "thirty yards of board fence nine feet high." It is a beautiful Saturday morning and all he wants to do is go off on "delicious expeditions" with other boys. Suddenly he gets an idea. Just as he guessed, soon a boy comes along and scoffs at him for having to work. Tom explains that he *likes* whitewashing. "Well, I don't see why I oughtn't to like it. Does a boy get a chance to whitewash a fence every day?" And so, very cleverly, he lures other boys into believing that it is an honor and a privilege to whitewash a fence. They end up doing the work for him as Tom sits on a barrel in the shade. It is a wonderful little episode, because Twain makes us see that this is exactly how human beings think and feel.

But there is much more in the book like how Tom and Huck turn up at their own funeral, how Tom rescues Becky Thatcher from the cave, and the stories of Injun Joe. It is a book packed full of adventures. It deserves all the fame it has gotten.

But it is also true that it is a sentimental book. Mark Twain knew how to make people laugh, but he also knew how to make them cry. Twain would now turn to a book that was not sentimental—the book that Ernest Hemingway said all American literature comes from.

Chapter 5
THE MASTERPIECE

MARK TWAIN WAS ALWAYS TELLING people that he was very lazy—it fit with the comical picture he liked to give of himself. In truth, he was a very hard worker, but he worked in spurts. He very much depended on the spirit of the moment. If the spirit moved him, he would write with great speed. When it didn't move him, he wouldn't write at all. He said,

Mark Twain at about age seventy, wearing the white suit that became his trademark. From boyhood Twain had liked showing off. The white suit made him stand out in a crowd.

65

As long as a book would write itself I was a faithful and interested amanuensis and my industry did not flag, but the minute that the book tried to shift to my head the labor of contriving its situations, inventing its adventures and conducting its conversation, I put it away and dropped it from my mind.

What this means is that Twain did not do a lot of thinking and advanced planning for his books. He would not force himself to think through a story so that everything would tie up neatly at the end. He counted on ideas flowing out of his mind. When they stopped flowing he stopped writing, instead of forcing himself to cast about for more ideas.

This way of working had a great advantage, because it meant that he wrote only when he had strong feelings about his subject. Those feelings shone through his work. But it also meant that he left many projects unfinished, because he wouldn't—or couldn't—work out ways to get them done.

This almost happened with his greatest work. In 1875, before *Tom Sawyer* was published, Twain wrote to a friend that he was thinking of writing a continuation of the Sawyer book, except that it would center on Tom's friend, Huckleberry Finn. In 1876 he sat down and wrote a considerable part of the book. Then he stopped. He explained, "I like it only tolerably well, as far as I have gone, and possibly may pigeonhole or burn the manuscript when it is done." He then worked on some other projects, especially a book about his riverboat days called *Life on the Mississippi*, today one of Twain's best-known books.

First editions of some of Twain's books that featured the Mississippi River. Twain had grown up along the great river, and it figured in his imagination for the rest of his life.

In 1883 he finally returned to the story of Huck Finn. It went along rapidly. The book was "writing itself," as Twain liked to put it, the ideas shooting out of his head in a steady stream. He said:

> *I haven't piled up [pages] so in years. . . . Why, it's like old times, to step straight into the study, damp from the breakfast table and sail right in & sail on, the whole day long, without thought of running short of stuff or short of words. . . . And when I get fagged out, I lie abed a couple of days & read & smoke & then at it again for six or seven days. He added, and I shall like it, whether anybody else does or not.*

Anybody interested in American writing, or any kind of writing at all, has to read *The Adventures of Huckleberry Finn*. Basically, it is the story of a boy who sees that the world around him is full of fakery and phoniness. Many of the people he meets pretend to be better or more important than they really are. Some try to seem wise but are always doing foolish things. Others follow the rules of polite society without noticing that some of them make no sense. Huck Finn exposes the deceits of society.

This is not surprising because Huck has always lived outside of society. He has no mother. His father is the town drunk and a disgrace. Eventually Huck runs away on a raft to ride down the broad Mississippi River with a runaway slave named Jim. Huck has grown up with slavery. Many of the people of his town own slaves. Like most Americans of the day, Huck has always believed that African Americans were inferior to whites—not as intelligent, lazy, and in general like children who have to be taken care of by their white masters.

Traveling down the Mississippi, Huck comes to know Jim well. He realizes that Jim is not lazy or stupid. In fact, readers soon come to see that Jim is morally a whole lot better than most of the white people in the story. Once again, Huck understands that a lot of what he has been told is not true.

Like most of Mark Twain's works, *The Adventures of Huckleberry Finn* does not have a straightforward plot.

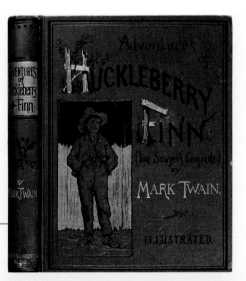

A first edition of Huckleberry Finn. *This was the cover the first readers of the great work saw.*

A historical sign demarking Cardiff Hill, where Twain set portions of both Tom Sawyer *and* Huckleberry Finn.

It is made up of various adventures that don't always relate to one another. At one point Huck and Jim get involved with a pair of tricksters who pretend that they are European aristocrats. Another time Huck gets caught up in a bloody feud between two families.

But the book is held together by the journey of the main characters, Huck and Jim. The center of the story is a moral question that keeps bedeviling Huck. He has been brought up to believe that slavery is *right*. Therefore, it is *wrong* for anyone to help a black slave escape. The slave, after all, is someone else's property, so helping him escape is like stealing. Stealing is a sin. In helping Jim escape, Huck is committing a sin and believes he is doomed to go to hell. Finally he decides that he mustn't commit a sin. He must tell on Jim. So he writes a note to Jim's owner. But when it comes down to it, he can't send the note to the owner. Huck's friendship for Jim is too strong. And so he says, "All right then, I'll *go* to hell." And he tears the note up.

It is one of the most moving and significant moments in American literature.

With *Tom Sawyer* and *Huckleberry Finn* Mark had finally established himself as the greatest American writer of his time. The mischievous boy from Hannibal, Missouri, who had begun life with little education and no money was now a star. He was admired by his fellow Americans who loved his books. He was now earning a great deal of money, although he lost some

By 1905, when Twain was seventy, he was famous not only in America, but elsewhere in the world. His seventieth year was celebrated by the very popular magazine Life with a cartoon of him on the cover.

of it on foolish investments. He lived in a grand house with a huge lawn and a coachman to drive him places, just as he had imagined all those years before when he was prospecting for silver. Famous people wanted to meet him, and when he traveled he was introduced to the mighty of other nations.

But at heart he remained that boy from Hannibal—indeed his wife, Olivia, often called him Youth. Even though he was now part of fashionable society, he continued to show up its foolishness in his books.

One book he did this in was *A Connecticut Yankee in King Arthur's Court.* It is certainly one of his best pieces. It is the story of a practical New Englander who wakes up suddenly to find himself in England back in the days of King Arthur. With his common-sensical views, he exposes the beliefs and superstitions of an earlier time, many of which still existed in Twain's day—and even today. Besides showing up myths and legends of King Arthur, the Connecticut Yankee brings into King Arthur's world modern inventions, like electricity and machine guns. *A Connecticut Yankee* starts out as a light, comic book, but grows in seriousness as it goes along. While he was writing it Twain himself said that the book had "slumped into funereal seriousness."

As he grew older, Mark Twain was more and more troubled by the evils he saw in the world. At the beginning of his career he wrote mainly humorous pieces, like his famous "Jumping Frog" story. Even *Tom Sawyer* was basically a light-hearted book, although it had its scary parts. Twain was able to laugh at the foolishness of people and the society they lived in.

But by the time Twain wrote *A Connecticut Yankee*, in the late 1880s, he was having trouble laughing at what he saw as the wrongs of human life. He had become pessimistic about the world. He had come to believe that human beings could be kind and decent to each other, but that often they were not.

As a result, he started writing essays and stories expressing this cynical viewpoint. Most Americans then liked to believe that things were always getting better. If they worked hard enough at doing good, the world could become a pleasant place. Mark knew that his pessimistic ideas would shock many of his readers. For one thing, many of his pieces spoke against religion. He decided that much of what he was writing at that time must not be published until some years after his death. Some of these dark stories and essays were not published until 1962, under the title, *Letters from the Earth*, a title Mark himself chose, for they would come from his grave. Anyone who wants to understand Mark Twain must read some of these dark pieces.

But it is the happier, comic stories we remember when we think of Mark Twain—the clever tricks of Tom Sawyer, the foolish frauds of the Duke and Dauphin who climb onto Huck's raft, the odd characters Mark meets in *Roughing It*, the deadpan manner in which the story of the celebrated jumping frog is told.

There is much more. Great writers are usually prolific. They are able to come up with one interesting character, one novel event, after another, seemingly without halt. Mark Twain went on writing interesting stories and essays almost to the moment of his death in 1910. He was seventy-five years old. But for another eighty years works by him would be discovered and published. What came out after his death would have made up a great body of work for a lesser writer.

We still read Mark Twain's books with pleasure today. Many of them have been made into movies, plays, and television shows. But none of these versions can capture the true humor of Mark Twain. For that you have to read the books.

A recent edition of A Connecticut Yankee in King Arthur's Court *used this illustration showing Twain meeting with the Connecticut Yankee of the story in a museum of ancient armor and weapons.*

TIME LINE

1835   Mark Twain is born in Florida, Missouri.

1839   Mark moves to Hannibal, Missouri.

1851   Mark begins work as a journeyman printer.

1857   Mark becomes a cub-pilot for Horace Bixby.

1861   The Civil War breaks out, halting river trade. Twain's life as a riverboat pilot is over.

1862   Mark travels around Nevada and California. He starts working as a repoter for the Virginia City *Territorial Enterprise*.

1870   Mark Twain marries Olivia Langdon (Livy) in Elmira, New York.

1876   Twain publishes *Tom Sawyer*.

1884   Twain publishes *The Adventure of Huckleberry Finn* in London. The American edition comes out the following year.

1910   Mark Twain dies at the age of seventy-five.

Author's Note on Sources

A tremendous amount has been written about Mark Twain. His life has been studied carefully and his books examined from many different viewpoints. A recent study of his work is *Mark Twain: A Literary Life*, by Everett Emerson (University of Pennsylvania Press: Philadelphia, 2000). A book concentrating on his youth and early life is *The Making of Mark Twain*, by John Lauber (American Heritage: New York, 1985). Some older books worth looking at are *Mr. Clemens and Mark Twain*, by Justin Kaplan (Simon and Schuster: New York, 1966) and *My Mark Twain*, by William Dean Howells (Harper & Bros.: New York, 1910). Howells was a major American writer of the time and was a close friend of Twain for some forty years. For students there are:

Mark Twain: A Writer's Life, by Milton Meltzer. Franklin Watts: New York, 1985.

Mark Twain: America's Humorist, Dreamer, Prophet, by Clinton Cox. Scholastic: New York, 1995.

INDEX

ABOUT THE AUTHOR

James Lincoln Collier has written many books, both fiction and nonfiction, for children and adults. His interests span history, biography, and historical fiction. He is an authority on the history of jazz and performs weekly on the trombone in New York City.

My Brother Sam Is Dead was named a Newbery Honor Book and a Jane Addams Honor Book and was a finalist for a National Book Award. *Jump Ship to Freedom* and *War Comes to Willy Freemen* were each named a notable Children's Trade Book in the Field of Social Studies by the National Council for Social Studies and the Children's Book Council. Collier received the Christopher Award for *Decision in Philadelphia: The Constitutional Convention of 1787.* He lives in Pawling, New York.